YES I HAVE ADHD #2. DEAL. W

Copyright © 2022 by Yes I Have Anxiety, Inc.

All rights reserved.

Thank you for purchasing an authorized edition of this book and for complying with copyright laws by not reproducing, scanning, or distributing any part of it in any form without permission.

Consumer Use Disclaimer: The "Yes I Have" book series was created in light-hearted, relatable fun to create distractions from things individuals may be dealing with. All "Yes I Have" books are not intended to diagnose medical conditions nor provide a cure for any medical conditions. This book is not meant to be a replacement for real medical intervention if needed.

ISBN: 978-1-958083-19-2
First Edition: May 2022
Yes I Have Anxiety, Inc.
Grove, Ok 74345

WHAT ARE YOU DEALING WITH?
WE GOT YOU!

Visit www.YesIHave.com for more books!

Do you have an idea for the next "Yes I Have®" book? Reach out to us through our website!

You might just see your idea in a future book!

What are you dealing with?

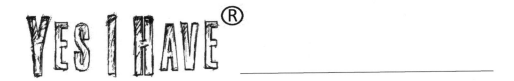

Make this Square Crazy.	Green Light! 
Fill the Battery. 	White out This Square.
Fill with Triangles.	Fill in the Black. 

Solve the Riddles!

| belt
hitting | loheadveheels | VIOL E T s | A B E DUMR | agb |

Give Him Hair!

Solve the Puzzle!

Sam and his friends all have favorite foods and drinks, and they are trying to decide where they can eat so that they can all have their favorites. Use the clues below to decide where each friend's favorite food and drink are.

1) Nancie's food can be pretty spicy and her drink is almost tasteless.
2) Nick likes to twirl his food around a fork. His drink come form different fruits.
3) Susie loves the cheesiness of her meatless food and the bubbliness of her drink.
4) Chrissy loves chicken nuggets. She also loves to drink
5) Tom's favorite food has a crunchy shell and he can see through his drink.
6) During warm months, **Sammy** sell her favorite drink at a stand.

	Pizza	Tacos	Spaghetti	Cheeseburgers	Chili	Chicken Nuggets	Lemonade	Cola	Water	Milk	Juice	Lemon-lime soda
Nancie												
Nick												
Susie												
Chrissy												
Tom												
Sammy												

Help the Chicken Lay Eggs all Over the Page!

Fill the Condiments!

Now put Them on the Hotdog!

Add Hair to the Hairless Cat!

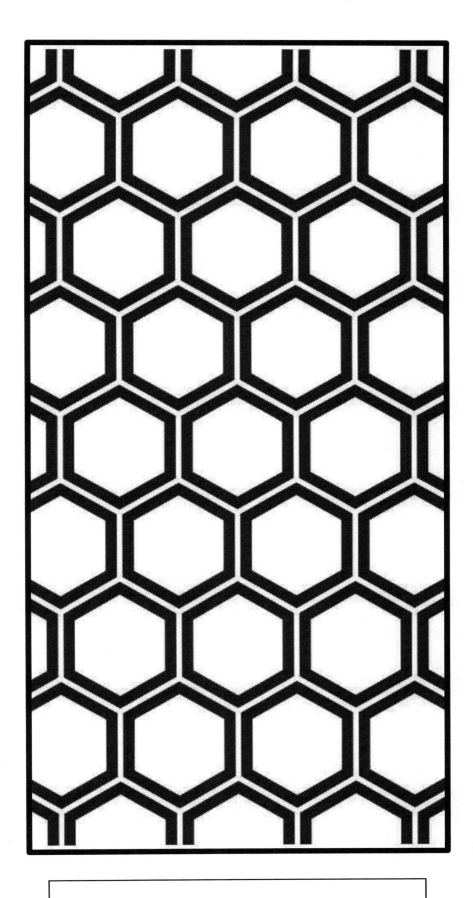

Just Color It.

Solve the Riddles.

arrest you're

r
o
rail
d

lu cky

go off coc

late nₑvₑr

world
world
world
world

k
pace

Write Your Name in Different Fonts on This Page!

Squiggle a Tornado.	Write Your Lucky Number.
Make This Square Blue.	This Square Needs Stripes.
Solve the Maze. 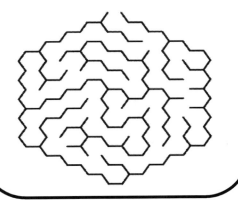	Make the Diamond Shine. 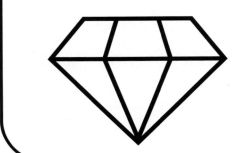

Are Rainbow Disco Balls a Thing?

Turn the Horse into a Unicorn!

Give the Lion a Mane!

Refresh Your Math Skills and Color the Picture!

Blue = 1 Green = 2 Yellow = 3
Orange = 4 Purple = 5 Pink = 6

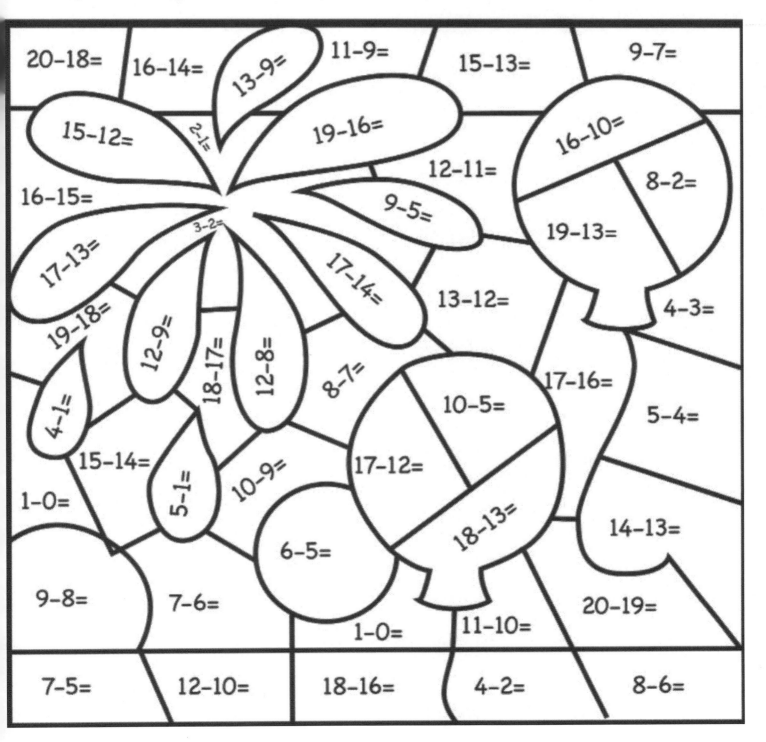

Make a Paper Chain Out of This Page!

P.S. Highlight These Letters!

C A
T

Add Vapor Lines from the Airplane in the Sky.

Complete the Story!

There are many _____ ways to choose a/an _____ to
            ADJECTIVE   **NOUN**

read. First, you could ask for recommendations from your friends and

_____ . Just don't ask your Cousin _____—she only
PLURAL NOUN   **PERSON IN ROOM (FEMALE)**

reads_____ books with _____-ripping muscle hunks
     ADJECTIVE   **ARTICLE OF CLOTHING**

on the cover. If your friends and family are no help, try checking out the

_____ Review in www._____press com. If the _____
NOUN   **A CITY**   **PLURAL NOUN**

featured there are too_____for your taste, try something a little
                          ADJECTIVE

more low-_____, like_____: A _____
       PART OF THE BODY   **LETTER OF THE ALPHABET**   **CELEBRITY**

interview, or _____Website. You could also choose a book the
               PLURAL NOUN

_____-fashioned way. Head to your favorite library or _____
ADJECTIVE   **A PLACE**

and browse the shelves until something catches your _____ .
                                                            PART OF THE BODY

Or, you could save yourself a whole lot of _____ trouble and log on
                                          ADJECTIVE

to www.bookfair.com, the _____ new website to _____ for
                               ADJECTIVE   **VERB**

books! With all the time you'll save not having to search for _____,
                                                                                PLURAL NOUN

you can read _____ more books!
                 NUMBER

Design a Cool Baseball Cap!

Turn the Circle into a Baseball!

What Scent? 	This Square Needs to be Rainbow.
Draw a Cloud.	Color This Square Red.
Draw a Sad Face.	Color the Cheese. 

Set a Timer for 1 Minute. How Many Four-Letter Words Can You Think of?

Design the Scrunchie!

What do your Charm Bracelets Say?

Color the Gummy Bears!

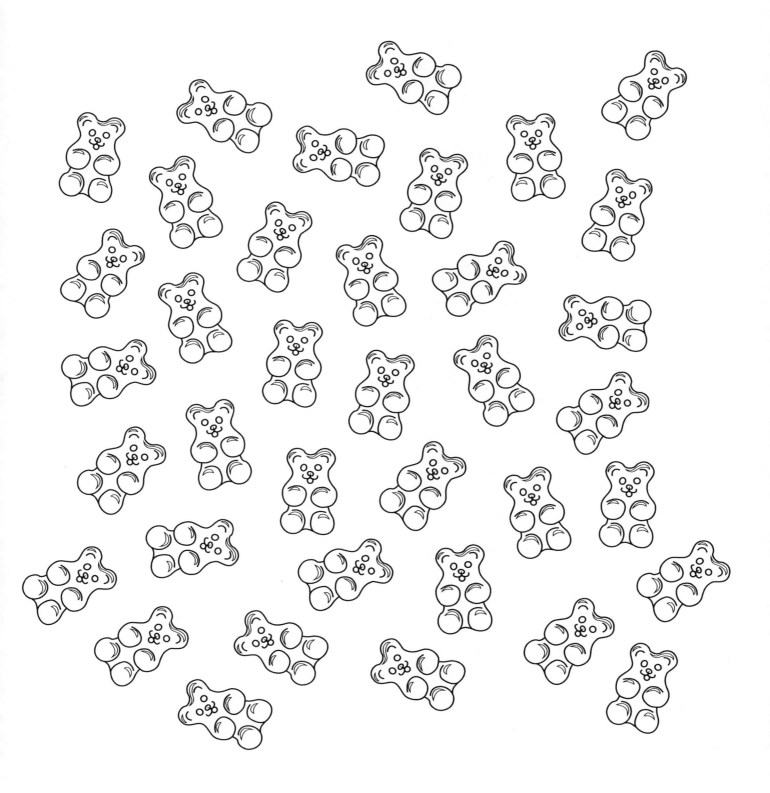

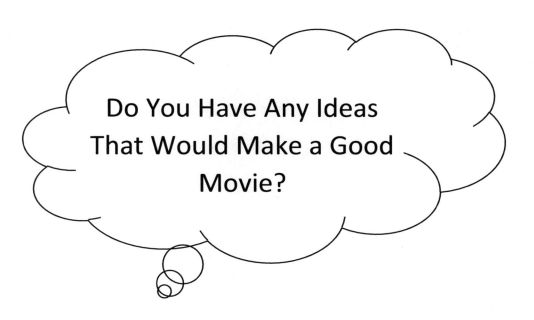

BRRR. Fill the Freezer with Ice Then Color the Popsicle.

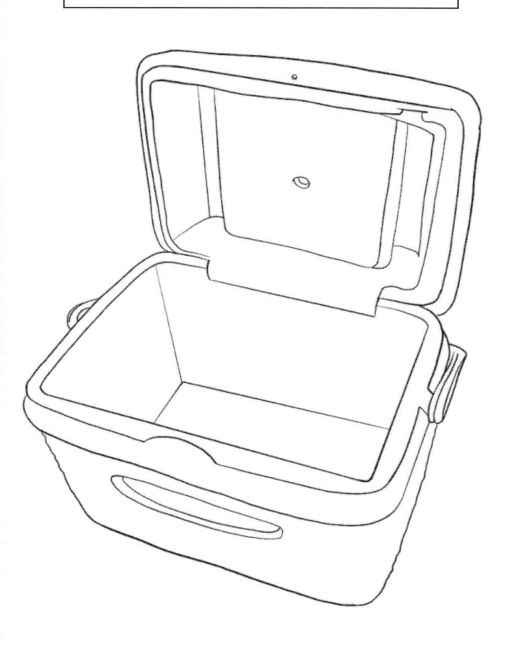

The Cherries Need Their Other Half!

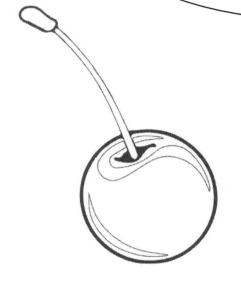
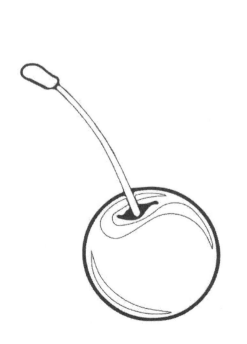

Paint This Page with a Toothbrush!

Make the Room Messy!

Add Jewels to the Crown.

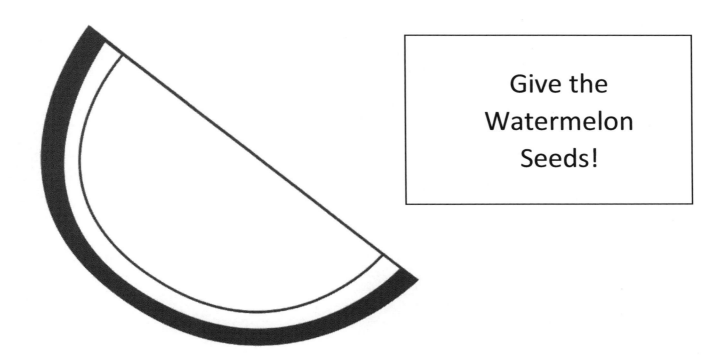

Give the Watermelon Seeds!

Draw a Rainbow.	This Square Needs to Sparkle.
What flavor? 	Color This Square Grey
Initial in This Box.	Color Her Eyeshadow. 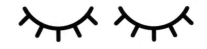

Make the Egg Yolk Run.

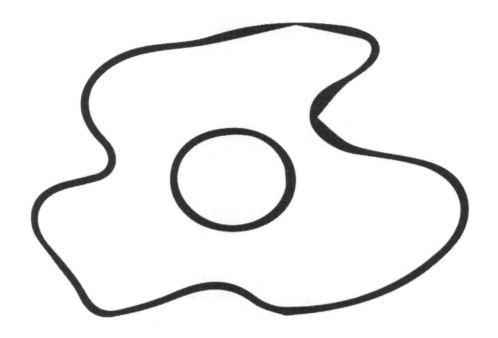

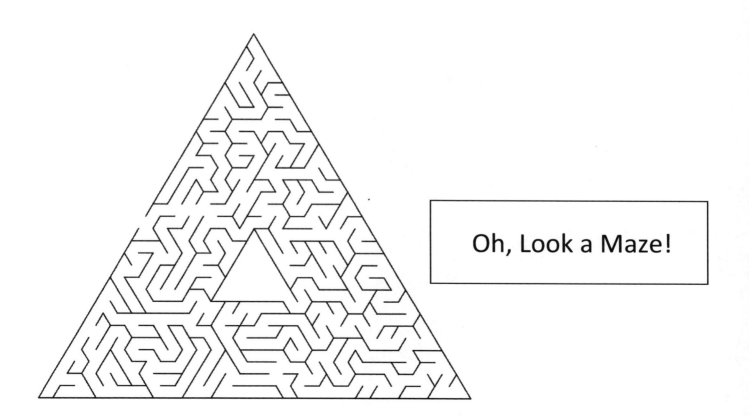

Oh, Look a Maze!

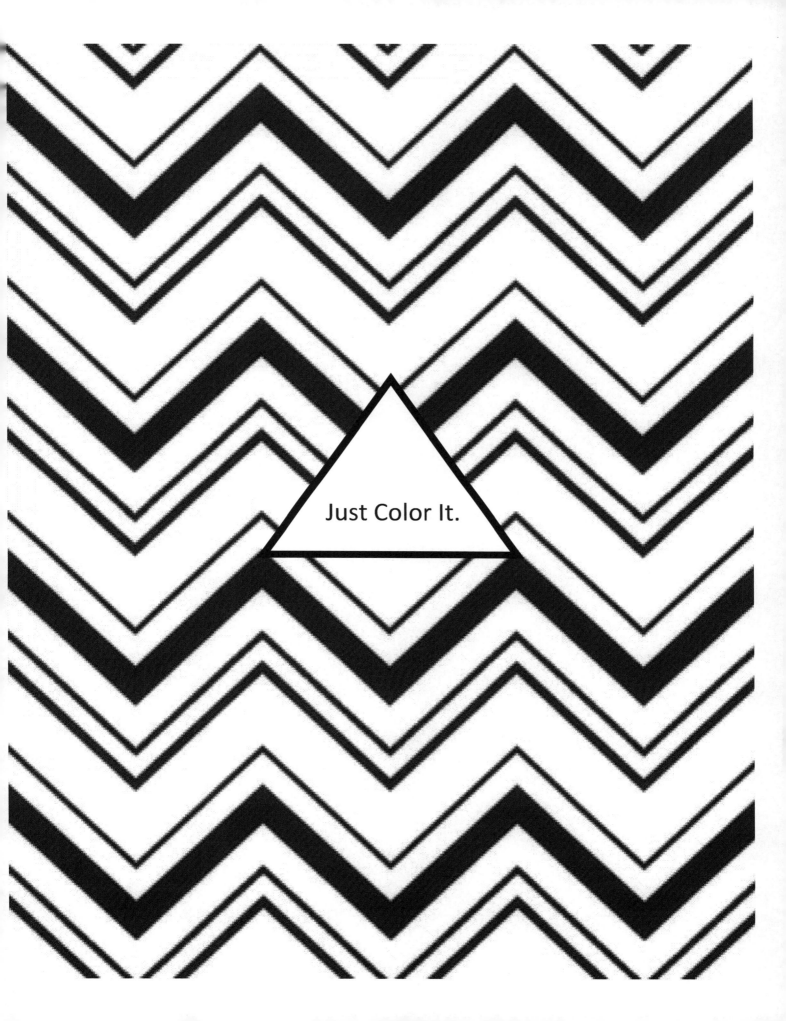

Write Yourself a Fortune.

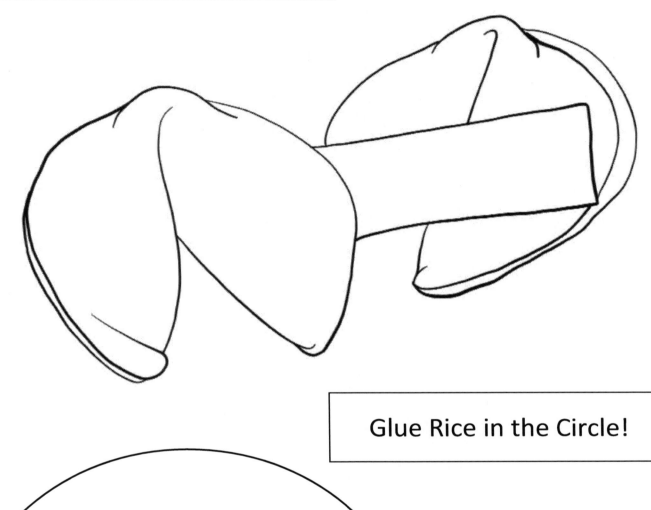

Glue Rice in the Circle!

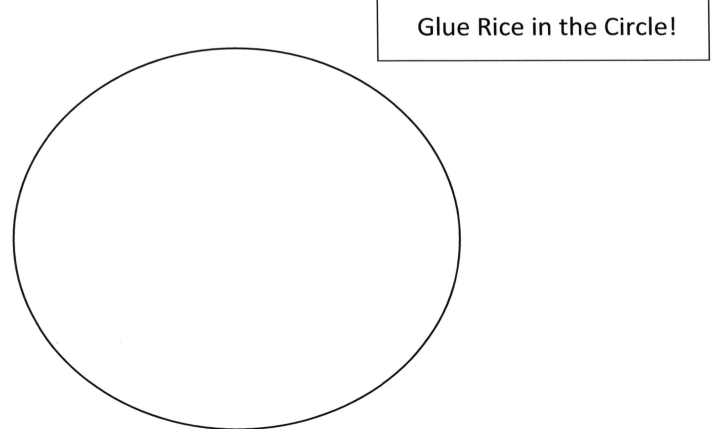

Customize These Shoes!

Oh No! The Fire Hydrant Broke. Make it Spray Water.

Fill in the Hopscotch!

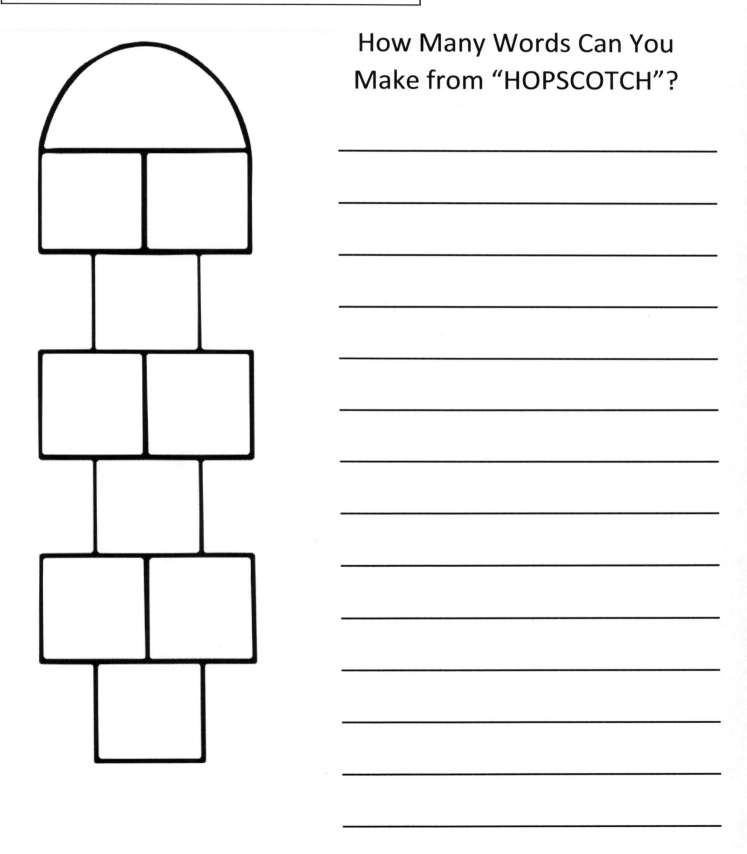

How Many Words Can You Make from "HOPSCOTCH"?

_____
_____
_____
_____
_____
_____
_____
_____
_____
_____
_____
_____

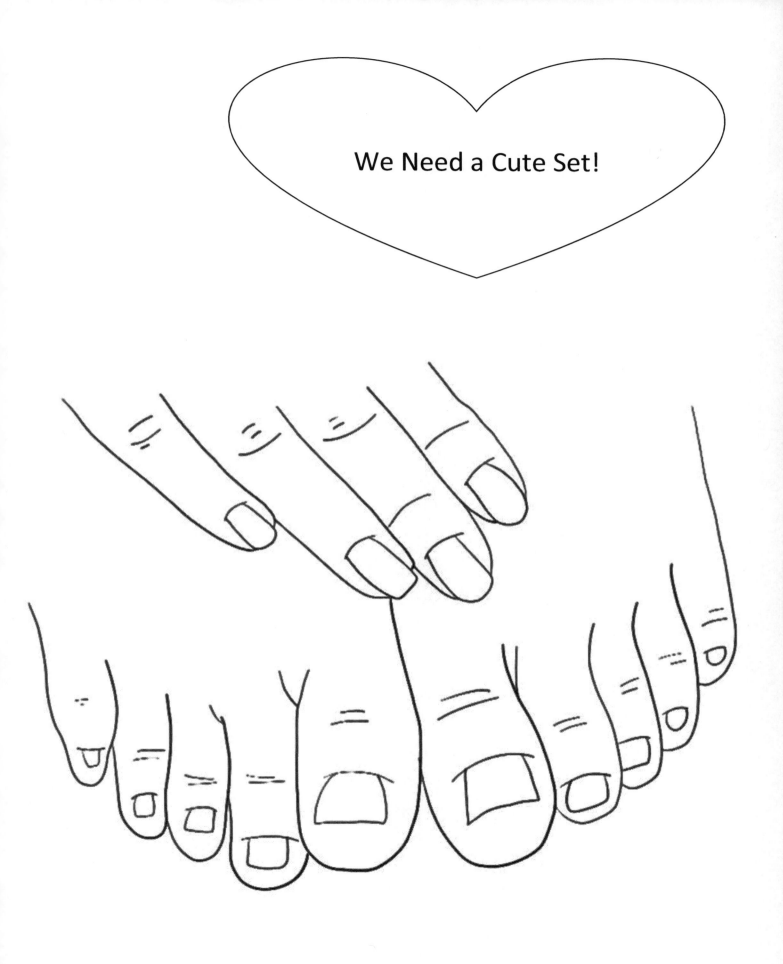

Make This Page Tie-Dye.

What are Your Favorite Movies?

What Does the Slime Look Like?

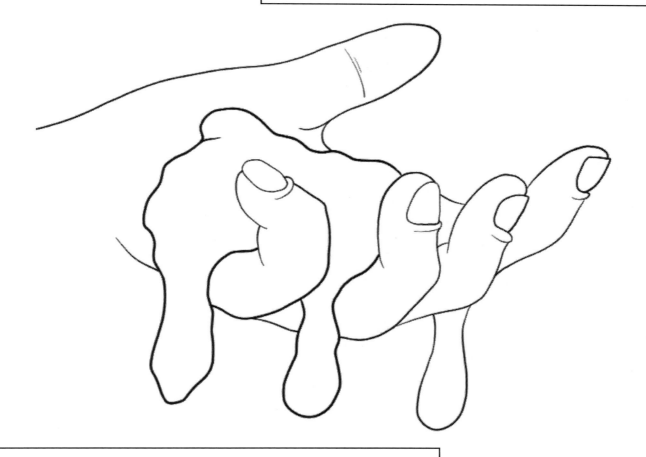

Solve the Riddles!

night fly	$_S{^T}{_I}{^N}{^K}$	injury + insult
dothepe	wear long	strich groound
the x way	word YYY	search and

Fix the Spelling.

1 twelf _____

2 forteen _____

3 too _____

4 fourty _____

5 fiveteen _____

6 sixtythree _____

7 ninty _____

8 tree _____

9 thriteen _____

10 eightteen _____

Solve These Riddles.

| you just me |
| cry
m i l k |
| o
TV |
| at the . of on |
| wor l |

What are Your Favorite Drinks?

What is Your Favorite Pie Flavor?

Draw a Tree.	Black out this Square.
Color the Butterfly 	Color This Square Purple
Draw a Cube.	Finish the Game. 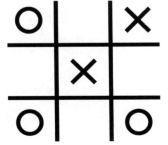

Design a Floorplan of Your Dream House!

Match the Pairs!

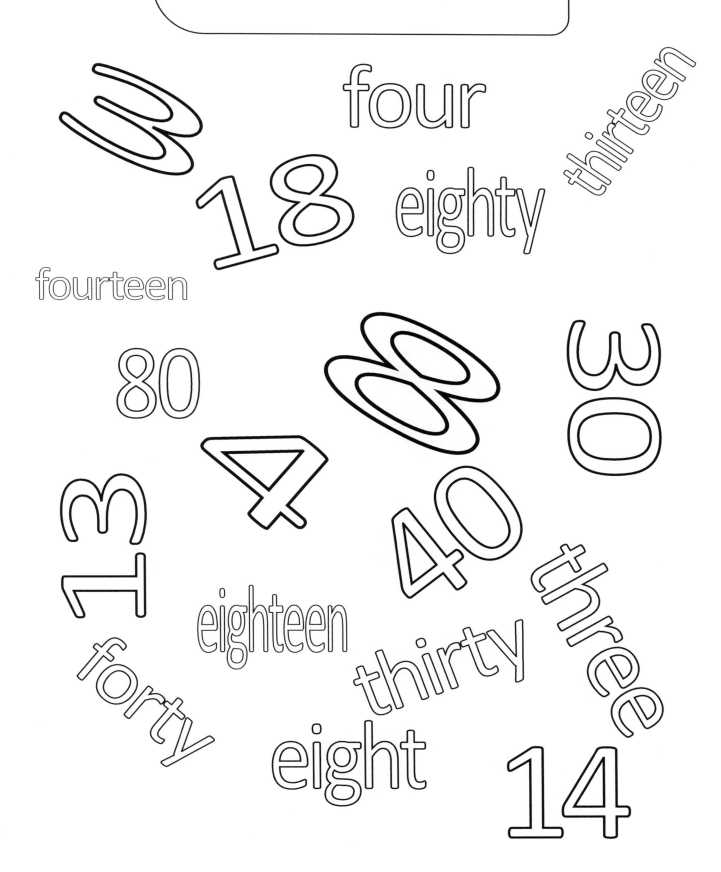

Color in the States You Have Been to!
Bonus Points if You can Name Them!

Add More Grapes to the Grapevine!

How Many Fruits Can You Find?

```
Y D N W O S T J F U B K S E P A R G C X
H R Z E M I L Y T C N A O T M V E L A R
M I E S J R W A V S O X P K Y F H N Q B
U C A B F Y N O M E L G E P R O A D T Z
L Q E X M G I F B H E R A U L N C W I S
P B Y T E U P K D O M V C J A E P H U A
G F A R N L C Z A S R N H B W T S E R F
X K I P R Z D U J Y E Q E M A N G O F W
R N L M H E Y Q C L T I S V H U B J E C
E O J G A W B M P X A O R X F K Z S P D
S T U C O F V P N Q W H L R O M T I A Y
B A E Y R K A X S Z F J D G E R V H R L
C M Y Q A E N H D A P M T L A B S R G I
J O L V N X F C I T R U S W D Q E Z K P
R T E I G P O S W E Y I B O N H T U J M
I S P D E N I R A T C E N F C J A X L O
Z W H U C Q M A G K R L U S G Y R E V B
A X I F L S J E B R D A P R I C O T N R
V G R K B H U P Y N J Z Q M L E W F D H
```

The Pigs Need Noses & Tails!

Don't miss out on FREE books and New Book Announcements!!!

Follow us on our social media platforms to be included in weekly giveaways, book tour location announcements, new book releases, and videos for page idea inspiration!!!

| officialyesihave | yesihaveofficial | Yes I Have Books | Yes I Have Official |

JOIN OUR NEWSLETTER!:
Text
YESIHAVE
To 22828 to get started!

Hey Fans!! If you post your page videos on social media and one goes viral, we want to know! Send your video to us at yesihavebooks@gmail.com

We showcase our viral fan videos on our website and social media outlets! We have 100+ viral videos and counting!

Want to Find More Books?

Scan the QR Code, Then Decorate it!

Mood Swings Perfectionism
Kids Anxiety Stress Ideas
Hard Times Pets Boredom
Baby Fever Christmas Fever

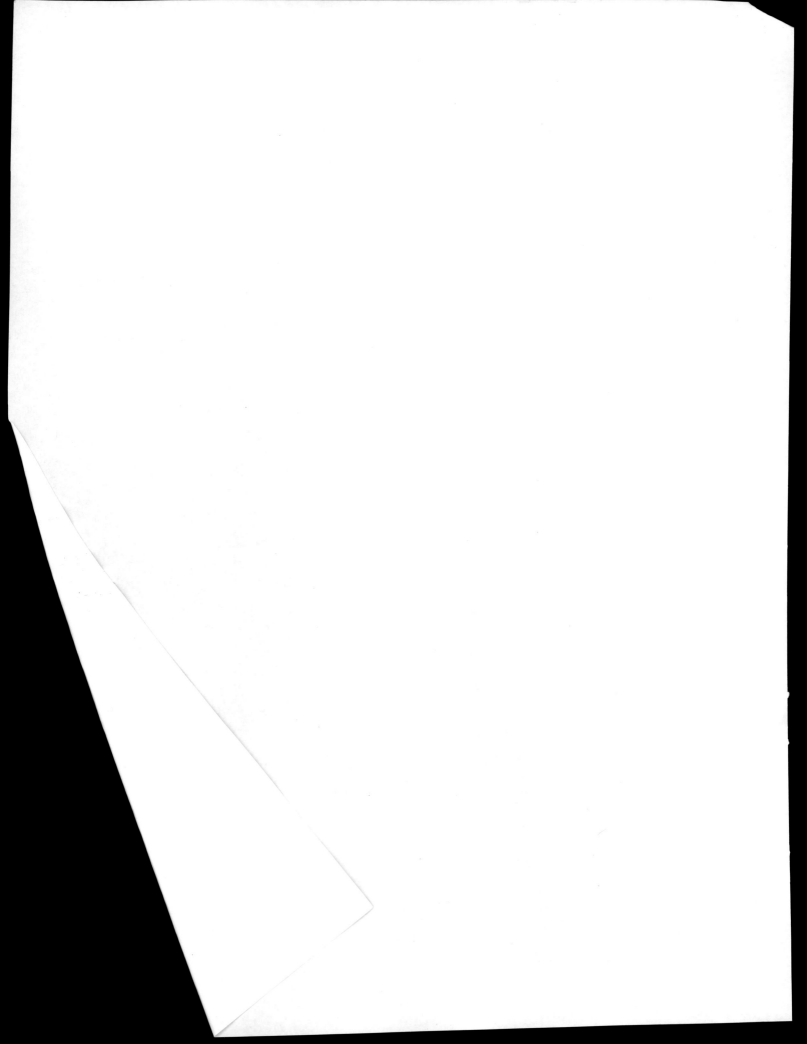